FRAGILE

ForgottenBee

Beeleevebooks

First Published by Beeleevebooks
2016 @beeleevebooks Somerset UK

The author asserts the moral right
under the Copyright, Designs and
Patents Act 1988 to be identified as
the author of this work.

ISBN: 978-0-9956420-1-0

A little slice of the physical in this ever
increasingly digital world.
You can hold me, hug me,
flick through my pages
and
I'll look fabulous on your bookshelf!

Introduction

'Bee Poem'

apis mellifera

Translucent frames filigree design,
hooks and grooves to swoop and wind.

Fresh floral scents beckon to follow their trail,
attraction strong of sense prevail.

For millions of years as the earth has revolved,
apis mellifera from vespa evolved.

Revered as a sedulous wonder of nature,
a driven force and health benefit creator.

Colonial living with strict roles to play,
odour distinct navigating their way.
200 beats per second and up to 15 miles per hour,
an average daily visit consists of 50-100 flowers.

With eyes of five and leg pairs of three,
they use polarized ultraviolet light to see.

This superorganism so much better organized,
than a top corporation.
Proves itself so essential to the food chain by its,
role in pollination.

Poem Title	Page Number

LIFE

LOVE

Poem Title	Page Number

LOSS

LIFE

somniare aestas

Laying back on the grass,
warm glow of the sun caresses,
ease of movement,
calm of composure.
Dreaming of summer

Smell of the salty air,
as out to sea we stare,
blue skies, gentle clouds drift.
Dreaming of summer

Another season yet to go,
as snow falls, time goes so slow,
heating on full blast.
Dreaming of summer

Alfresco dining until late,
flowers of the garden a picture create,
worries seem less.
Dreaming of summer

This season still remains
gales, frosty mornings, heavy rain,
as we awake to the gloom.
Dreaming of summer

Rhythm Heat

Always creating the high,
as rhythm and stamina fly,
the pounding beat,
pedal, plate thumping feet.

Fanning snaps and sweeps,
jazzy brush techniques,
with hands that stir the passion
accent the beat the cymbal crashing.

Tssh...TTssh...TTtssh the hi-hat
takes the stage,
the constant pulse, the heartbeat wave,
then comes the resonant bass,
punching depth, a constant pace.

Excitement builds, groovy fills and licks,
energy rising,
thumping beats and kicks.

To the instrumental break,
driving spang-a-lang for the swing jazz zone.
Percussion sticks take a turn,
as their sexy rhythmic chops,
smoke a burn.

Flesh and Blood

A pool of blood,
A bucket of sweat,
A flood of tears,
in the raising of you I've shed.

Did I not bite my lip?
As blaming vengeful
words at me you spit!

The hateful eye you cast my way,
as again I refuse to pay
for yet more unnecessary shit!

Forgotten patience and hugs,
endless worries discarded.
As you threaten to leave
unable to get your own way.

"Work harder, get a job, stop living like a slob!"
Stealing money from my purse
like an albatross, a curse.

Laughing at my ways
and how ancient my ideas,
'til the moment you learn I'm right,
and how hard for you I'll always fight.

You are my flesh and blood!
Which for me means
endless forgiving love.

amans vitae

A drawing, a place
the lines upon your face,
that knowing look, my favourite book,
a rainbow, a tear,
scent of a flower near.
A desperate need, a fear finally freed,
your hands on my back, that perfect track.
Warm words, lustful embraces,
exciting tingles,
hot party mingles.
Nakedness!
Freshly mown grass, delicious tastes
kisses on my face.
Full bodied wine
dinner alfresco, crunching snow
new people to know.
Successful endeavours,
dancing all night,
music played loud, feeling proud.
Silence to hear.
Addictive smells, being understood,
a walk in the woods.
Presents to give, energy shared,
believing in me, countries to see
artwork revered,
tiny creatures,
clear blue skies,
endless loving in your eyes!

Toast

Toast. I love you the most
when your edges are crisp,
teeth clattering bliss.

Toast. I love you the most
with butter not jam,
or tomato sauce and ham.

Toast. I love you the most
when not a soggy mess,
all limp and lifeless.

Toast. I love you the most
when you pop up and say 'hi'
lightly golden, the smell I sigh!

Toast, I love you the most
when hunger takes a grip,
you're warm and quick.

Toast. I love you the most,
next to my egg neatly trimmed,
dipped in my soup, I watch you swim.

Toast. I love you the most
not charcoal burnt, check the gauge
I've learnt.

Toast. I love you the most
you just simply satisfy, I can't lie!

Sock Disa'pair'ance

There's a sock on the stair,
it should be in a pair!
How did it get there?
When the other is elsewhere!

There's a sock on the stair,
I walk past it in despair,
it should be in a pair!
With my other underwear.

There's a sock on the stair,
an odd occurrence I declare,
they're always in a pair!
Why it's not is rather rare.

There's a sock on the stair,
it should be in a pair!
Of the other I'm not aware,
and to be honest I don't care!

There's a sock in my bra?
Oh! There you are!

complexus

'Morning',
please don't have already arrived!
I'm tired and can barely open my eyes.
Let me stay in this foetal position,
my body won't move, and to my head
won't listen.

Yet through the curtains,
I can feel the sun's rays.
Persuading me gently,
to face the chill and embrace the day.

I need an excuse, something tangible
to stay in bed.
I reach across and still feel the pillow
indented by your head.

You, like me don't want to rise!
Don't want to wake, and open your eyes.

Only one thing left then,
that we can possibly do.
Is under the covers have
a cuddle or two!

On Fire

I love the days, when productivity's ablaze.
As slowly the hands on the clock creep,
and the more you achieve.

No lost for words, or unable to write.
Just the energy coursing,
as pen to paper unite.

Doors open, and forthright you walk in.
Never questioning why?
or where to begin.

The phone keeps ringing, you answer the calls.
Rising to challenges,
confidence high, avoiding pitfalls.

Even late into the night, you keep on going.
As that adrenaline spike,
in the bloodstream is still flowing.

Sleeping is problematic,
as you struggle to close your eyes.
Through your head, ideas are rushing.
All aimed to blow the skies.

Then it's the next day,
which takes a different gear.
Now, you're really in control
of the life you steer!

Familiar

I sit here,
you sit there,
we stare.

Bow of Hues

Open the curtains
and the day begins,
the colour of the sky
the mood brings.
Grey and cloudy
not a great beginning,
mist lifting day remains,
you'll be winning.

Then there's the drizzle
with a dark tinge,
wetting the masses
at the train station they whinge.
Lack of coat as it started out fine,
sudden change,
in need of shelter we whine.

Snow in April!?
What happened to showers?
Caught under canvas,
it's been raining for hours.
Too hot, and I'm sweltering,
how many layers?
Leaves on the track and now they delay us!

Christmas day arrives, and will it snow?
Chances of that we already know!
Sadly, as always it's wind and rain,
then an electrical storm,
thunder and lightning again.

Hail denting cars,
they're as big as golf balls.
Frost sticking firm,
early starts for all.

Endless rain,
flooding the fields and towns,
bringing trouble to communities,
terrible destruction found.

Thick fog on the motorway!
Limited vision as we drive.
Wind speeds increasing,
pushing the cars
from side to side.

Wind combined with rain,
turning umbrellas inside out.
Season blending into season,
heat rising bringing droughts.

Hose pipe bans
and the sun keeps shining!
For weeks and weeks,
so comes a silver lining.
Gentle showers increasing to more,
creating a bow of hues,
we gaze in awe and adore.

vanitas

with uncurled fingers, and outstretched arm,
thin skinned,
paper like,
wrapping around bones,
creaking, groaning,
in her frenzied palm.

the eerie temptress
comes to call
with talons deep
sunk in them all

green eyes a flash light strike,
to hypnotise,
disguise aesthetics,
as lured on promises the siren's song
lulls through high pitched tones,
building images that tantalise,
enticing them to fantasise.

the eerie temptress
comes to call
with talons deep
sunk in them all

in plain view under moon beams gaze,
the musty toadstool under foot,
the rising stench of stale waters living years.
and those that pass are unaware,
of how she further tightens her hold,
draining their life force in her skeletal grip,
as on her thick dripping sweet talk they sip.

life

the eerie temptress
comes to call
with talons deep
sunk in them all

hidden in trees on moss ridden stones,
lurking deep the boggy mire,
her whispers beckon, slippery their sagacious prose.
eagerly encompassing,
violently seducing,
with inveigle into her deadly bosom plucked.

the eerie temptress
comes to call
with talons deep
sunk in them all

devouring motive, impenetrable shield,
guzzling on the fresh innocence of unspent days,
freely, easily, she sucks the power of will,
until all that's left are
egos driven to beguile.

the eerie temptress
comes to call
with talons deep
sunk in them all

instincts vigour propels veracious
words to warn,
as with nefarious strikes, she cuts the ties
of heart over mind, avaricious her motive.
so keep selfless, true, the soul
then from the temptress's
icy shackles you'll fall.

Insomnia

Challenging the sheep,
as my eyes open
mid sleep.

From the depths
I leap,
abruptly back to reality.
Confused, bewildered,
now awake,
and unable to again fall asleep.

The calm,
the quiet,
the early morning
the those still snoring.
The mid dream awakening,
open eyes,
the birds sing.

'Savage Beauty'

*Short poems written on a coach returning
from London inspired by Alexander McQueen
V & A Exhibition 2015*

Each stitch, each button sewn,
with intricate skill,
to challenge the viewer
and give the wearer free will.
-
Seductive layers,
cuts made with power.
Designs breaking rules
formed to empower.
-
Zips and buckles, fur lace and feathers.
Crystal headdresses, flesh peeping leather.
-
Openings, slits, back flattering waists.
Sharp, angular, animalistic,
boundary pushing taste.
-
Tortured, challenging images created,
erotica deliciously animated.
-
The theatrics of design,
the elaborate,
the grotesque,
goading the divine.

Grammarsow

In darkness
beneath the floors
between the walls
I crawl.
Dampness surrounds me.
Musky smells cover me.
At night,
an orgy!
Legs over legs
as we feast on rotting death.
Over each other we fall,
armored shelled,
curling into a ball,
as under rocks we crawl.

LOVE

anima mate

Even if you're not always there,
in my mind I know you care.

With you I want to be

When we cross words because it's late,
and I shout over you when I should wait.

With you I want to be

When I lose my positivity,
and expose my vulnerability.

With you I want to be

When I take the defensive part,
about something close to my heart.

With you I want to be

When you see me at my worst,
and just because in tears I burst.

With you I want to be

When I worry too much about others,
yet believing in me again suffers.

With you I want to be

love

When a life time I've struggled hard,
and been dealt some awful cards.

With you I want to be

When I'm feeling really low,
and my insecurities start to grow.

With you I want to be

When I want to feel strong and brave,
be cheeky, naughty and misbehave.

With you I want to be

Because

*you accept
the real me.*

Unbridled Passion

I lie here contemplating,
as I breath in and out.
Feeling my chest rise and fall,
what were we about?

A mistake?
Did we rush and jump in head first?
No thought of the future,
just our loins about to burst.

And then in a flash,
that moment comes to an end.
Leaving a canvas so muddied
the loss of a best friend.

Was it worth the pain?
At the time I'd say yes!
Safe within your arms,
tight together undressed.

But that's all we had!
There was nothing more!
No deeper attraction
than our flesh to explore.

So let's part with a smile and
think fondly on this,
unbridled passion,

wanton feelings of bliss.

love

Feeling 16

'Feeling 16'!
Loves young dream,
but the heartache
sometimes can be extreme.

A new start,
made so hard when we're apart.

The excitement,
the buzz,
the just
two of us.

The learning you!
You
learning me too!

When our lips smouldering meet,
that feeling of being complete.

Skin to skin,
a deeper closeness begins.
The nerves kicking in,
each time we meet again.

Despite the life we've already seen,
together we're still 'Feeling 16'!

The Power of a Kiss

Soft and gentle, a soul revealed.
Lips meeting together, a promise sealed.
Light yet deep,
an aching heart may weep.

Strengthening spirit and mind,
freeing anxiety to calm and unwind.

Completed senses,
overcoming defenses.

Passion drawn from within.
Desire raised to sin.
Unable and unwilling to stop,
the more it continues the more inhibitions drop.

A picnic in the park,
a walk after dark,

a chance meeting,
a friendly greeting.

And yet!

To never embrace and accept the power,
of how such a touch can weaken, and devour,
would make an empty lonely life,
that only looks to embrace, trouble and strife.

love

At the Edge of the Sea

Under the moonlight would
you dance with me?
Entwined senses,
touches,
minds running free.

To the rush of the waves
would you play your guitar?
That song you wrote,
for me from afar.

Would you instinctively know
my want, my need?
Feel my passion,
my lustful greed.

Then under the moonlight
would you make love to me?
Consume my desire
at the edge of the sea.

tempore

Time,
that constant tick,
as languidly together we sit.

And watch,
and watch,
as people pass by.
The endless motion of the hands fly.

A gentle move as fingers link,
skywards eyes lock.
Clouds drift, and reflect,
on the face of the clock.

Time,
that constant tick,
as languidly together we sit.

love

primum tempus

The awkwardness and building of nerves,
but backing out now, would be absurd.
Questioning decision made!?
Yet, adrenaline rushing,
quickly, makes indecision fade.

Appearance surely shouldn't be top?
Humour and kindness, count for a lot.
Yet, shallow I must definitely be!
As I still hope, and want to like what I see!
Worrying now, about their height.
And whether from description they're
recognizable on sight.
Yet, what if they change their mind on me?
And turn around instinctively!
But, it might turn out to be the perfect time!
A connection made, whilst sharing the wine.

So, go with the flow and come what may.
At the end of the date,
you can always walk away!

Letting Go

When I reflect on now,
and how I got here somehow.
I think of loves past,
life's shadows cast.

All consuming,
unfolding,
driving pain,
letting go.

Awkward moments of silence,
the nervousness of new.
The fire of lust,
the need to just see it through.

All consuming,
unfolding,
driving pain,
letting go.

Baring body and soul,
yet never feeling the whole.
Jealousy kicking in,
as desire starts wearing thin.

All consuming,
unfolding,
driving pain,
letting go.

love

Broken hearts and fragility,
friendships lost and stability.
Downsizing house,
loss of revenue.
Losing confidence and ability.

All consuming,
unfolding,
driving pain,
letting go

Then just when you have given up,
resigned to be alone, and out of luck.
Along comes that unique, special one,
with open mind and so much fun.

All desiring,
feeling free,
loving gain,
completing me.

Office Crush

As she leant across the desk
his heart began to race,
his eyes wandered to her chest
instead of connecting with her face.

She loved to be a tease
in the way she moved her hips.
And she could sense his unease,
as her pencil touched her lips.

She sat taking notes,
her leg across her knee.
He couldn't help but dote,
on all that he could see.

Dictation now complete
she moved to leave the room,
he jumped up to his feet,
to stop her leaving him too soon.

love

Sports Shop Encounter

To the local sports shop
she made a trip.
With the positive endeavour
to get herself fit!

As she scanned the shelves
for the perfect footwear.
She could sense the
shop assistant's, transfixed stare.

A vision of beauty
was all he could see.
The goddess of his dreams,
running section aisle three!

Swiftly he moved
in her direction.
Planning to impress, with his sales
patter suggestions.

She sensed his intent, panicked,
wanted to hide. So unconfident with her
looks, into the running pants she dived!

Bemused he decided to hover by the till,
his feelings to declare as she paid her bill.

Disheveled she emerged crawling
on all fours. She made her escape,
but got trapped between the sliding doors.

love

SOS my Heart

Leaving me stranded, SOS my heart.
Then just like you planned it,
shipwrecked from the start.

A chance meeting at the station.
Your pursuit of seduction overpowered me.
How could I know such adoration,
came at a price I'd not yet sec.

Leaving me stranded, SOS my heart.
Then just like you planned it,
shipwrecked from the start.

Soulmates together, believing nothing
could ever falter. A love that forever
my core worshipped at the altar.

Leaving me stranded, SOS my heart.
Then just like you planned it,
shipwrecked from the start.

At your touch I fall,
to your draw my body submits.
How could you close the door on it all?
When we were such a perfect fit!

Leaving me stranded, SOS my heart.
Then just like you planned it,
shipwrecked from the start.

love

So here I nurse the pain,
the tension created became the art.
Broken hearted again,
pushed together driven apart.

Leaving me stranded, SOS my heart.
Then just like you planned it,
shipwrecked from the start.

LOSS

papilionem

Winged spiritual messenger,
possess magical fragility,
dancing on the breeze,
with such whimsical tranquility.

Shape shifting transformation,
metamorphosis begins.
Power of soul evolution,
in the form of angels wings.

A symbol from the grave,
ethereal existence on earth,
induces power to be brave,
embrace the joy,
and freedom of worth.

esuritio

If you take my hand,
I'll lead you out of the darkness,
act as a light to show you the way.

Your fears deathly hold,
with trust, are challenged with might.
Together our strength, a powerful fight.

Courage of mind, and force of will,
weakness defies, and blackness withholds.

With tightness of grip,
desire, want, and passion to live,
future goals to pursue,
from this lonely void,
you'll pull through.

Forgiving You

I think too much and analyse,
bringing up complicated
thoughts I despise.
Bad versus good.
Forgive you I should!

It's a hard thing to do,
after everything I've been through.
But the positivity I possess,
should be enough to confess.
And forgive you!

So much given and taught,
knowledge shared,
and challenges brought.
I faced them all with strength!
So forgive you I ought!

Passing time brings the new,
changes for a whole, and brighter view.
Future built free from experiences past.
Forgive you I do!

Widow's Lament

Time is a healer, or so they say.
The seconds, the minutes,
the hours,
slip by.

Days become weeks,
weeks become months,
yet the pain,
still remains.

The silence is deafening!
Expectations to still feel
and sense a presence.
Yet flowers decay, dried and withered
by the elements.

The emptiness collects,
the tears and words,
of the widow's lament.

Nights loneliness, days of quiet
insomnia takes hold.
Regrets. What ifs?
Conversations never had,
unable to forgive.

Yet the end, creates a new start.
As a circle completes,
and the pain lessens,
its hold on the heart.

loss

So time is a healer, or so they say!
Never forgotten,
the spirit kept alive in memories.

A vigil, at your side, kept once a year.
Laughter to again fill the house,
as the happy times resume,
and a new future of possibilities bloom.

The Bench Lies Empty

Sitting on the terrace,
a perfect summer day,
is how I like to remember us,
before you went away.

Too painful to remember,
memories close to the heart,
time will never heal them,
now we are apart.

Under the sheets I hide,
away from realities trace,
there my dreams are endless,
there I see your face.

And so the bench lies empty,
I can't bear to sit alone!
Curtains drawn, windows closed,
outside world blocked.
I've lost my home!

Space to Breath

You gave me space,
a time to breath.
To help me realise,
thoughts and needs.

Scarred at first,
I felt alone.
Yet, after time,
thoughts became my own.

More and more,
independence grew.
My attitude changed,
in everything I knew.

The freedom you permitted,
to fulfil your own.
Helped to shape me,
my confidence full grown.

So now that you've returned,
after your experimental time.
You no longer fit
with the desires and thoughts of mine.

absque

I understand why, each time you
have to leave.
But, my heart feels heavy, and I can
hardly breath.

The emptiness inside,
so difficult to bear.
Every time I look out of the window,
and your car's no longer there.

Keeping my mind busy,
and remaining strong.
Is the way I get through every day,
and manage to move on.

Then time quickly passes and
again I see your face,
the memory of us parting,
is readily erased.

Old of Spirit

How could she have known?
How could she have foreseen?
When tomorrow came,
he'd no longer waken from his dream.

So young, yet old of spirit,
wisdom well beyond his years.
His demons finally caught him,
he embraced them shedding fears.

Sometimes it's just a moment,
in our lifetime with someone.
His journey may have ended,
but hers has just begun!

The End

scribo

The words flowed easily, from
her head to the paper,
as a liquid suspended
in the air,
as a vapour.

Narratives created to thrill
and inspire.
Thrillers with twists,
romance fuelled by desire.

Fictional characters,
forged from reality.
Having to face in print,
their own mortality.

New worlds created,
a special place of her own.
Friendships, and lovers,
the power to never be alone!

About the Poet

Born in Greenwich London,
ForgottenBee began to
write poetry from a very
young age, finding that it
helped her to work through
emotions, and over time
reflect upon her life experiences.

This is her first poetry book
which includes a collection
of poetry under three sections
'life, love and loss'.

Several of the poems
have been recorded using
'Spoken Word' and uploaded
to SoundCloud. Many of which
have been mixed by musicians
for their music and feature on
EPs and albums.

Bee has now found her
creative home living in Somerset.

Twitter:- @forgottenbee
FaceBook:- www.facebook.com/forgottenbee
SoundCloud:- www.soundcloud.com/forgottenbee
Blog:- www.forgottenbeeblog.wordpress.com
BeeleeveBooks Twitter:- @beeleevebooks

www.ingramcontent.com/pod-product-compliance
Lightning Source LLC
Chambersburg PA
CBHW071103040426
42443CB00013B/3394